Why Jesus?

Nicky Gumbel

Illustrated by
Charlie
Mackesy

Published in North America by Alpha North America
1635 Emerson Lane, Naperville, IL 60540
© 2008 by Nicky Gumbel

This edition issued by special arrangement with Alpha International,
Holy Trinity Brompton, Brompton Road, London SW7 1JA, UK

Why Jesus?
by Nicky Gumbel

Originally published by Kingsway Publications Ltd, Lottbridge Drove,
Eastbourne, East Sussex, England BN23 6NT

First printed by Alpha North America in 2001

Printed in the United States of America

Unless otherwise stated, Scripture quotations taken from the Holy Bible,
New International Version® Anglicized, NIV® Copyright © 1979, 1984,
2011 Biblica, Inc.® Used by permission. All rights reserved.

Scripture quotations marked (AMP) taken from the Amplified Bible 2015,
Copyright © by The Lockman Foundation, La Habra, CAS 90631. All
rights reserved.

Scripture marked (MSG) taken from The Message Copyright © 1993,
1994, 1995, 1996, 2000, 2001, 2002 by Eugene H. Peterson.

Illustrations by Charlie Mackesy
ISBN 978 1 938328 91 6

1 2 3 4 5 6 7 8 9 10 Printing/Year 21 20 19 18 17

What's it all about?

Relationships are exciting! They are the most important aspect of our lives—our relationships with our parents, boyfriend or girlfriend, husband or wife, children, grandchildren, friends, coworkers, and so on.

Christianity is first and foremost about relationships rather than rules. It is about a Person more than a philosophy. It is about the most important relationship of all—our relationship with the God who made us. Jesus said that the first and greatest commandment is to love God. The second is to love our neighbor. So, it is also about our relationships with other people.

Why do we need him?

You and I were created to live in a relationship with God. Until we find that relationship

there will always be something missing in our lives. As a result, we are often aware of a gap. One rock singer described it by saying: "I've got an emptiness deep inside."

A woman, in a letter to me, wrote of "a deep deep, void." Another young girl spoke of "a chunk missing in her soul."

People try to fill this emptiness in various ways.

Some try to close the gap with money—but that does not satisfy. Aristotle Onassis, who was one of the richest men in the world, said at the end of his life, "Millions do not always add up to what a man needs out of life."

Others try drugs or excess alcohol or sexual promiscuity. One girl said to me, "These things provide instant gratification but they leave you feeling hollow afterwards." Still others try hard work, music, or sports, while others seek success. There may not be anything wrong with these in themselves but they do not satisfy that hunger deep inside every human being.

Even the closest human relationships, wonderful though they are, do not in themselves satisfy this "emptiness deep inside." Nothing will

fill this gap except the relationship with God for which we were made.

According to the New Testament, the reason for this emptiness is that men and women have turned their backs on God.

Jesus said, "I am the bread of life" (John 6:35). He is the only one who can satisfy our deepest hunger because He is the one who makes it possible for our relationship with God to be restored.

a) He satisfies our hunger for meaning and purpose in life

At some point everyone asks the question, "What am I doing on earth?" or, "'What is the point of life?" or, "Is there any purpose to life?" As Albert Camus once said, "Man cannot live without meaning."

Until we are living in a relationship with God we will never find the true meaning and purpose of life. Other things may provide passing satisfaction but it does not last. Only in a relationship with our Creator do we find the true meaning and purpose of our lives.

b) He satisfies our hunger for life beyond death

Before I was a Christian I did not like to think about the subject of death. My own death seemed a long way in the future. I did not know what would happen and I did not want to think about it. I was failing to face up to reality. The fact is that we will all die. Yet God has "set eternity in the hearts of men" (Ecclesiastes 3:11). Most people do not want to die. We long to survive beyond death. Only in Jesus Christ do we find eternal life. For our relationship with God, which starts now, survives death and goes on into eternity.

c) He satisfies our hunger for forgiveness

If we are honest, we would have to admit that we all do things that we know are wrong. Sometimes we do things of which we are deeply ashamed. More than that, there is a self-centeredness about our lives which spoils them. Jesus said, "What comes out of you is what makes you 'unclean.' For from within, out of your hearts, come evil thoughts, sexual immorality, theft, murder, adultery, greed, malice, deceit, lewdness, envy, slander, arrogance and folly. All these evils come from inside and make you 'unclean' " (Mark 7:20-23).

Our greatest need, in fact, is for forgiveness. Just as someone who has cancer needs a doctor whether they realize it or not, so we need forgiveness whether we realize it or not. Just as with cancer, those who recognize their need are far better off than those who are lulled into a false sense of security.

By His death on the cross

Jesus made it possible for us to be forgiven and brought back into a relationship with God. In this way He supplied the answer to our deepest need.

Why bother with Jesus?

Why should we bother with Christianity? The simple answer is because it is true. If Christianity is not true, we are wasting our time. If it is true, then it must be of vital importance to every human being.

But how do we know it is true?

We can test the claims of Christianity because it is an historical faith. It is based on the life, death, and resurrection of Jesus Christ. Our faith is based on firm historical evidence.

Who is Jesus?

Jesus is the most remarkable man who ever lived. He is the centerpiece of our civilization. After all, we call what happened before Him B.C. and what happened after Him A.D.

Jesus was and is the Son of God. Some people think He is just a "good religious teacher."

However, that suggestion does not fit with the facts.

a) His claims

Jesus claimed to be the unique Son of God—on an equal footing with God. He assumed the authority to forgive sins. He said that one day He would judge the world and that what would matter then would be how we had responded to Him in this life.

C. S. Lewis pointed out, "A man who was merely a man and said the sort of things Jesus said would not be a great moral teacher." He would either be insane or else he would be "the devil of hell." "You must make your choice," he writes. Either Jesus was, and is, the Son of God or else He was insane or evil but, C. S. Lewis goes on, "let us not come up with any patronizing nonsense about His being a great human teacher. He has not left that open to us. He did not intend to."

b) His character

Many people who do not profess to be Christians regard Jesus as the supreme example of a selfless life. Dostoevsky, himself a Christian, said, "I believe there is no one lovelier, deeper, more sympathetic and more perfect than Jesus. I say to myself, with jealous love, that not only is there no one else like him but there could never be anyone like him."

As far as His teaching is concerned, there seems to be general agreement that it is the purest and best ever to have fallen from human lips.

To C. S. Lewis it seemed clear that Jesus could neither have been insane or evil and thus he concludes, "however strange or terrifying or unlikely it may seem, I have to accept the view that he was and is God."

c) His conquest of death

The evidence for the physical resurrection is very strong indeed. When the disciples went to the tomb on the first Easter day they found that the grave clothes had collapsed and that Jesus' body was absent.

In the next six weeks He was seen by over 500 people. The disciples' lives were transformed and the Christian Church was born, and then grew at a dynamic rate.

A former Lord Chief Justice of England, Lord Darling, said of the resurrection, "In its favor as living truth there exists such overwhelming evidence, positive and negative, factual and circumstantial, that no intelligent jury in the world could fail to bring in a verdict that the resurrection story is true." The only satisfactory explanation for these facts is that Jesus did indeed rise from the dead and thus confirms that He was, and is, the Son of God.

Why did he come?

Jesus is the only man who has ever chosen to be born and He is one of the few who has chosen to die. He said that the entire reason for His coming was to die for us. He came "to give his life as a ransom for many" (Mark 10:45).

From what we know of crucifixion, it was one of the cruelest forms of execution. Cicero described it as "the most cruel and hideous of tortures." Jesus would have been flogged with a whip of several strands of leather weighted with pieces of metal and bones. According to Eusebius, a third-century historian, "The sufferer's veins were laid bare, and the very muscles, sinews and bowels of the victim were opened to exposure."

Jesus was then forced to carry a six-foot cross beam until He collapsed. When He reached the site of execution, six-inch nails were hammered through His wrists and feet as He was nailed to the cross. He was left to hang for hours in excruciating pain.

Yet, the New Testament makes it clear that there was something worse for Jesus than the physical and emotional pain; this was the spiritual anguish of being separated from God as He carried all our sins.

Why did he die?

Jesus said He died "for" us. The word "for" means "instead of." He did it because He loved us and did not want us to have to pay the penalty for all the things that we had done wrong. On the cross He was effectively saying, "I will take all those things on myself." He did it for you and He did it for me. If you or I had been the only person in the world He would have done it for us. St. Paul wrote of "the Son of God, who loved me and gave himself for me" (Galatians 2:20). It was out of love for us that He gave His life as a ransom.

The word "ransom" comes from the slave market. A kind person might buy a slave and set him free—but first the ransom price had to be paid. Jesus paid, by His blood on the cross, the ransom price to set us free.

Freedom from what?

a) Freedom from guilt

Whether we feel guilty or not, we are all guilty before God because of the many times we have broken His laws in thought, word, and deed. Just as when someone commits a crime there is a penalty to be paid, in the same way there is a penalty for breaking God's law. "The wages of sin is death" (Romans 6:23).

The result of the things we do wrong is

12

spiritual death—being cut off from God eternally. We all deserve to suffer that penalty. On the cross Jesus took the penalty in our place so that we could be totally forgiven and our guilt could be taken away.

b) Freedom from addiction

Jesus said that "everyone who sins is a slave to sin" (John 8:34). Jesus died to set us free from that slavery. On the cross, the power of this addiction was broken. Although we may still fall from time to time, the power of this addiction is broken when Jesus sets us free. That is why Jesus went on to say that "if the Son sets you free, you will be free indeed" (John 8:36).

c) Freedom from fear

Jesus came so that "by his death he might destroy him who holds the power of death—that is, the devil—and free those who all their lives were held in slavery by their fear of death" (Hebrews 2:14-15). We need no longer fear death.

Death is not the end for those whom Jesus has set free. Rather it is the gateway to heaven, where we will be free from even the presence of sin. When Jesus set us free from the fear of death, He also set us free from all other fears.

Freedom for what?

Jesus is no longer physically on earth but He has not left us alone. He has sent His Holy Spirit to be with us. When His Spirit comes to live within us, He gives us a new freedom.

a) Freedom to know God

The things which we do wrong cause a barrier between us and God: "your iniquities have separated you from your God" (Isaiah 59:2). When Jesus died on the cross He removed the barrier that existed between us and God. As a result He has made it possible for us to have a relationship with our Creator. We become His sons and daughters. The Spirit assures us of this relationship and He helps us to get to know God better. He helps us to pray and to understand God's Word (the Bible).

b) Freedom to love

"We love because he first loved us" (1 John 4:19). As we look at the cross we understand God's love for us. When the Spirit of God comes to live within us we experience that love. As we do so we receive a new love for God and for other people. We are set free to live a life of love—a life centered around loving and serving Jesus and loving and serving other people rather than a life centered around ourselves.

c) Freedom to change

People sometimes say, "You are what you are. You can't change." The good news is that with the help of the Spirit we *can* change. The Holy Spirit gives us the freedom to live the sort of lives that deep down we have always wanted to live. St. Paul tells us that the fruit of the Spirit is "love, joy, peace, patience, kindness, goodness, faithfulness, gentleness and self-control" (Galatians 5:22-23). When we ask the Spirit of God to come and live within us, these

wonderful characteristics begin to grow in our lives.

Why not?

So God offers us in Christ Jesus forgiveness, freedom, and His Spirit to live within us. All this is a gift from God.

15

When someone offers us a present, we have a choice. We can either accept it, open it, and enjoy it. Or else we can say, "No thank you." Sadly, many people make excuses for not accepting the gift which God offers.

Here are some of the excuses:

a) "I have no need of God"

When people say this they usually mean that they are quite happy without God. What they fail to realize is that our greatest need is not "happiness" but "forgiveness." It takes a very proud person to say that they have no need of forgiveness.

We all need forgiveness. Without it we are in serious trouble. For God is not only our loving Father; He is also a righteous judge.

Either we accept what Jesus has done for us on the cross, or else one day we will pay the just penalty ourselves for the things we have done wrong.

b) "There is too much to give up"

Sometimes, God puts His finger on something in our lives that we know is wrong and that we would have to give up if we want to enjoy this relationship with God through Jesus.

But we need to remember:

16

- God loves us. He asks us only to give up things that do us harm. If I saw some small children playing with a carving knife I would tell them to stop, not because I want to ruin their fun but because I do not want them to get hurt.

- What we give up is nothing compared to what we receive. The cost of not becoming a Christian is far greater than the cost of becoming a Christian.

- What we give up is nothing compared to what Jesus gave up when He died on the cross for us.

c) "There must be a trap"

Understandably, people often find it hard to accept that there is anything free in this life. They think it all sounds too easy and that there must be some hidden trap. However, what they fail to realize is that although it is free for us, it was not free for Jesus. He paid for it with His own blood. It is easy for us but it was not easy for Him.

d) "I'm not good enough"

None of us is good enough. Nor can we ever make ourselves good enough for God. But that is why Jesus came. He made it possible for God to accept us just as we are, whatever we have done, and however much of a mess we have made of our lives.

e) "I could never keep it up"

We are right to think that we could never keep it up. We cannot by ourselves, but the Spirit of God, who comes to live within us, gives us the power and the strength to keep going as Christians.

f) "I'll do it later"

This is perhaps the most common excuse. Sometimes people say, "I know it's true but I'm not ready." They put it off. The longer we put it off, the harder it becomes and the more we miss out. We never know whether or not we will get another opportunity. Speaking for myself, my only regret is that I did not accept the gift earlier.

What do we have to do?

The New Testament makes it clear that we have to do something to accept the gift that God offers. This is an act of faith. John writes that "God so loved the world that he gave his one and only Son, that whoever believes in him shall not perish but have eternal life" (John 3:16).

Believing involves an act of faith, based on all that we know about Jesus. It is not blind faith. It is putting our trust in a Person. In some ways it is like the step of faith taken by a bride or a bridegroom when they say, "I will" on their wedding day.

The way people take this step of faith varies enormously but I want to describe one way in which you can take this step of faith right now. It can be summarized by three very simple words:

a) "Sorry"

You have to ask God to forgive you for all the things you have done wrong and turn from everything which you know is wrong in your life. This is what the Bible means by "repentance."

b) "Thank you"

We believe that Jesus died for us on the cross. You need to thank Him for dying for you and for the offer of His free gift of forgiveness, freedom, and His Spirit.

c) "Please"

God never forces His way into our lives. You need to accept His gift and invite Him to come and live within you by His Spirit.

If you would like to have a relationship with God and you are ready to say these three things, then here is a very simple prayer which you can pray and which will be the start of that relationship.

Lord Jesus Christ,

I am sorry for the things I have done wrong in my life (take a few moments to ask His forgiveness for anything particular that is on your conscience). Please forgive me. I now turn from everything which I know is wrong.

Thank You that You died on the cross for me so that I could be forgiven and set free.

Thank You that You offer me forgiveness and the gift of Your Spirit. I now receive that gift.

Please come into my life by Your Holy Spirit to be with me forever.

Thank You, Lord Jesus. Amen.

What now?

1. Tell someone

It is important to tell someone in order to underline the decision you have made. Often it is only when you tell someone else that it becomes a reality to you. It is probably best to start by telling someone who you think will be pleased to hear the news.

2. Read the Bible

Once we have received Jesus and put our trust in Him we become children of God. He is our heavenly Father. Like any father He wants us to have a close relationship with Him. We develop this relationship as we listen to Him (primarily through the Bible) and as we speak to Him in prayer. The Bible is the word of God and you might find it helpful to begin by reading a few verses of John's gospel every day. Ask God to speak to you as you read.

3. Start to speak to God each day (ie pray)

I find the following a great help:

A - Adoration
Praising God for who He is and what He has done.

C - Confession
Asking God's forgiveness for anything that we have done wrong.

T - Thanksgiving
Thanking God for health, family, friends, and so on.

S - Supplication
Praying for ourselves, for our friends, and for others.

4. Join a lively church

It is important to be part of a group of Christians who get together to worship God, to hear what God is saying to them, to encourage one another, and to make friends. Church should be an exciting place!

I first prayed a prayer like the one on page 21 on February 16, 1974. It changed my life. It is the best and most important thing I have ever done. I trust it will be the same for you.

Go Deeper
with
Bible In One Year

bibleinoneyear.org

Bible in One Year is a free daily Bible reading resource with commentary by Nicky and Pippa Gumbel. Each day a passage from the Old Testament, a Psalm or Proverb, and a passage from the New Testament are covered so in the course of one year, the whole Bible is read. Intended to be read or listened to alongside the Bible to provide fresh understanding of the texts, it is available via email, with the Bible in One Year app, and online at bibleinoneyear.org.

Since its development in 2009, Bible in One Year has had over a million unique downloads and subscriptions in 194 countries, many of these readers coming from Alpha.

The fifth session of Alpha explores the question, "How and why should I read the Bible?" and Bible in One Year is introduced as part of this. Thousands of Alpha guests worldwide, many of whom have never before read the Bible, have already found this to be a simple, practical and inspiring resource to deepen their growing faith.

The following pages are selected excerpts from Bible in One year for you to consider:

Your Trial Will Become Your Triumph
Taken from Bible in One Year—Day 150

"Houston, we've had a problem," were the words of Jim Lovell on the evening of April 13, 1970. Nearly fifty-six hours into the mission to the moon, an explosion aboard the spacecraft plunged the crew into a fight for their survival. Within less than a minute there was a cascade of systems failures throughout the spacecraft. "It was all at one time – a monstrous failure," said NASA's flight controller.

The spacecraft looped around the moon, using its gravity to return to earth. Millions of people followed the drama on television. Eventually, the capsule splashed down in the Pacific Ocean near Tonga.

"Although the mission was not a success from a conventional perspective, it was a *triumph* of ingenuity and determination," wrote Paul Rincon, science reporter for the BBC in an article headed *Apollo 13: From Disaster to Triumph*. Jim Lovell said it showed the people of the world that *even if there was a great catastrophe, it could be turned into a success.*

The supreme example of triumph coming out of apparent catastrophe is the cross. What seemed to the world to be the ultimate defeat was in fact the ultimate triumph.

Psalm 68:21–27
1. Triumph of God

As we look around at the world today we see so much evil – the fanatical atrocities of ISIS, Boko Haram and other evil regimes and organizations.

This psalm celebrates God's ultimate triumph over evil and, in particular, evil nations and empires. You are invited to watch the *triumphal* entry of God into his temple. God has *triumphed*. Right has won the day. Human pride and inflated arrogance will one day be humbled before the majesty of God's just rule.

David describes a triumphal procession celebrating the victory of God over his enemies: "Surely God will crush the heads of his enemies... your procession has come into view, O God, the procession of my God and King." (vv.21,24)

There follows a picture of the worshipping community as it should be, with singers, musicians, tambourines and more, all praising God – and with the princes among them (vv.24–27).

Lord, I pray that we would see a revival of worship and that the leaders of our nation would be at the heart of worshipping communities, praising God in the great congregation (v.26).

New Testament
John 19:1–27
2. Triumph of Jesus

Have you been through hard times in your life? Perhaps you are in the middle of hard times right now and things aren't looking good in your life at this moment. Remember that at the time of his greatest triumph it did not look good for Jesus.

I remember talking to Father Raniero Cantalamessa, Preacher to the Papal Household, just before he took part in a public debate with one of the "New Atheists." I asked Father Raniero whether he thought he would win. He replied that he did not know. He said he might lose the debate. "But," he added, "God can be glorified in defeat."

The crucifixion of Jesus shows that God can be glorified in what appears to be a defeat. This is the moment of Jesus' greatest triumph.

Three times Pilate protested that Jesus was innocent (18:38; 19:4–6), and on two further occasions he tried to get out of allowing Jesus' death (see also 19:12,14). But in the end he was too weak to act as his conscience led. He "caved in to their demand. He turned him over to be crucified." (v.16, MSG)

Jesus' death was entirely voluntary. No longer free to move, Jesus was, in fact, the only one who was totally free. Pilate said, "Don't you realize I have power either to free you or to crucify you? (v.10) Jesus answered, "You haven't a shred of authority over me except what has been given you from heaven." (v.11, MSG) The irony was that Jesus had total authority over Pilate.

This was the hour of great darkness. Jesus was flogged, a crown of thorns was put on his head, he was struck in the face, he was handed over to be crucified, he was stripped of his clothes and the soldiers cast lots for his undergarments. Yet through it all, the Scriptures were being fulfilled (vv.23–24).

John emphasizes the fulfillment of prophecy and the royalty of Jesus. Throughout Jesus' trial and crucifixion, there is the constant theme of whether he is a king. The soldiers dress Jesus up as a mock king and shout, "Hail, *king* of the Jews." (v.3) Pilate declares with bitter irony, "Here is your *king*," (v.14) and asks, "Shall I crucify your *king*?" (v.15) The chief priests reply, "We have no *king* but Caesar," (v.15) and so Pilate has a sign prepared stating: "Jesus of Nazareth, the *king* of the Jews." (v.19)

As Jesus is being crucified, he looks anything but a king. He is being taunted and mocked. Yet, the irony is that as Pilate organizes for the notice to be prepared (in three languages so everyone can read it, v.20), God's purposes are being fulfilled in proclaiming to the whole world that *Jesus is God's King*. He is the King of Love, hidden and silent.

During his trial, Jesus declared to Pilate, "You are right in saying that I am a *king*." (18:37). However, unlike Caesar, his kingdom is "not of this world," (v.36) for it is an eternal heavenly kingdom. This eternal King is *triumphing*, not through the might of Roman *triumphalism*, but through the seeming weakness of death on a cross.

Jesus is triumphing over darkness, evil and sin. Tomorrow we will read those great words, "It is finished." (19:30) Jesus completed the task of bearing the world's sins in his own body. The greatest victory in the history of the world had been won. This is the triumph of good over evil, of life over death.

His life appears to be a horrible failure. Hate seems to have conquered love. But in fact, the conquered one, who has apparently failed, has in fact triumphed and opened up a source of new life, a new vision for humankind and a new road to peace and unity.

If you are struggling at the moment with the circumstances of your life, stay close to Jesus and remember that God can be glorified in defeat. The greatest triumphs in our lives sometimes occur when the circumstances seem to be hardest.

Lord, thank you that because of your triumph God always leads us in triumphal procession in Christ, and 'through us spreads everywhere the fragrance of the knowledge of him' (2 Corinthians 2:14).

Old Testament
1 Samuel 26:1–28:25
3. Triumph of David
David's triumph does not come easily. Victories in life are rarely easy. They generally come after many difficulties and failures.

Saul said to David, "May you be blessed, my

son David; you will do great things and surely *triumph*." (26:25)

It is tragic to see how far Saul had fallen. At one stage he was the Spirit-filled man of God, getting rid of evil from the land. Now he finds himself consulting the very witches he has expelled (chapter 28). Yet verse 19 suggests that even in the Old Testament there were the beginnings of the knowledge of life after death, and that in spite of all he had done, the Lord saved Saul – "tomorrow you and your sons will be with me." (28:19)

We also see the worst side of David's character. He joins the Philistines, lives by deceit and murders women and children (chapter 27). He has to sink to the lowest depths to hide what he is doing. The picture the Bible paints of David is far from perfect, and yet God uses him despite his failings and failures.

On the other hand, we also see David at his best. David had an opportunity to take revenge on Saul, who was trying to kill him. However, David refused to take revenge. He had great respect for Saul, because he was in a position of authority.

He says, "Who can lay a hand on the Lord's anointed and be guiltless?… The Lord forbid that I should lay a hand on the Lord's anointed." (26:9,11)

David stayed loyal and faithful to Saul despite the fact that Saul was trying to murder him. Follow David's example and refuse to be led into sin in an attempt to break free of a person's authority over you.

Even Saul recognizes David's 'righteousness and faithfulness' (v.23). Saul sees that he "will do great things and surely *triumph.*"(v.25)

The life of David teaches us not to expect instant success and triumph. Often, God prepares us through the years of obscurity, difficulty and even defeat or failure. It is in these times of testing that, like David, we must not act out of revenge but rather with love, honor and respect.

Lord, thank you that you use us powerfully in spite of our many failings. Thank you that our triumph over evil is only possible through the triumph of Jesus on the cross and in his resurrection.

Pippa Adds
John 19:25-27

I can't imagine what Mary the Mother of Jesus was going through as she stood watching her son dying on the cross. It was bad enough when one of our children broke a leg and another had to have an operation. Watching your children suffer is the most painful thing. Mary is an inspiration as a mother, and the love between mother and son is so touching.

Jesus' concern and provision for his mother at this most difficult moment of his life is a reminder of the importance of caring for our families.

Notes:

Paul Rincon, 'Apollo 13: From Disaster to Triumph', [Online] http://news.bbc.co.uk/1/hi/sci/tech/8613766.stm [last accessed December 2014].

How to Feel God's Love For You
Taken from Bible in One Year—Day 199

"Feel" is a song by Robbie Williams in which he writes, "I just wanna feel real love." God wants you to *feel* his love for you. He wants you to accept his love in your heart. You can receive his love in a new way today.

I remember an occasion when our grandson, aged two, wanted to feel his father's love. He raised both hands in the air and said, "Hugga Dadda." My son picked up his son, lifted him into his arms, embraced him, kissed him and hugged him. It is a wonderful thing to hold a father's hand but an incomparably greater thing to have his arms wrapped around you. This is an illustration of the experience of God's love.

We *know* that God loves us through the cross: "God demonstrated his own love for us in this: While we were still sinners, Christ died for us." (Romans 5:8) We *experience* God's love through the Holy Spirit: "God has poured out his love into our hearts by the Holy Spirit, whom he has given us." (5:5)

"The whole Bible," St Augustine observes, "does nothing but tell of God's love." Raniero Cantalamessa writes: "This is the message that supports and explains all the other messages. The love of God is the answer to all the 'whys' in the Bible: the why of creation, the why of the incarnation, the why of redemption. If the written word of the Bible could be changed into a spoken word and become one single voice, this voice, more powerful than the roaring of the sea would cry out: 'the Father loves you!' (John 16:27). Everything that God does and says in the Bible is love, even God's anger is nothing but love. God 'is' love!"

Psalm 86:11–17
1. God's love is great and personal
When you know the greatness of God's love for you the response is worship: "I will praise you, O Lord my God, with all my heart; I will glorify your name forever." (v.12)

David knew it was the love of a personal God who cares for each individual. He writes, "For great is your love towards me." (v.13a) Like David, you are God's "dear, dear child!" (v.16, MSG)

It is God's nature to love. "But you, O God, are both tender and kind, not easily angered, immense in love." (v.15, MSG) He prays, "Make a show of how much you love me." (v.17, MSG) He prayed, in the light of God's love for him, for an "undivided heart." (v.11b) He wanted to respond to God's love for him by committing himself totally to God.

Lord, you are compassionate and gracious, abounding in love and faithfulness (v.15). Thank you that your love for me is so great and so personal. Give me an undivided heart.

2. God's love is demonstrated and poured out

Do you believe that God really loves you? God's love will never let you down; he will never stop loving you. His love for you is greater than your failings and he wants you to receive his love by faith.

Contrary to what many people think, God loves you and wants to give you *life*. He gives *"life* to the dead." (4:17) God raised Jesus to life from the dead. One day all who have died, in Christ, will also be given resurrection life. In the meantime, Jesus said that he came so that you might experience life, and life in all its fullness. (John 10:10)

Paul continues to describe Abraham's faith. Abraham believed God's promise that he and Sarah would have a child, even though it was no longer a human possibility.

We learn of Abraham that "no unbelief or distrust made him waver (doubtingly question) concerning the promise of God, but he grew strong and was empowered by faith as he gave praise and glory to God, fully satisfied and assured that God was able and mighty to keep His word and to do what He had promised." (Romans 4:20–21, AMP) In other words, Paul reiterates, Abraham was justified by faith.

But justification by faith was not only for Abraham, "but also for us, to whom God will credit righteousness – for us who believe in him who raised Jesus our Lord from the dead." (v.24) You too are justified by faith. "The sacrificed Jesus made us fit for God, *set right with God.*" (v.25, MSG)

Paul moves on to speak of the staggering consequences of this fact. Because you are "justified by faith," you have "peace with God." You have "gained access" to his presence. (5:1–2, MSG) You can draw near to him and speak to him each day, knowing that there is no barrier between you and him.

"There's more to come: We continue to shout our praise even when we're hemmed in with troubles." (v.3, MSG) We can rejoice in our sufferings: "Because we know that suffering produces perseverance; perseverance, character; and character, hope. And hope does not disappoint us, because *God has poured out his love into our hearts by the Holy Spirit*, whom he has given us." (vv.2–5)

God's love has flooded your innermost heart. This experience of God's love is deep and overwhelming. It is the regular ministry of the Holy Spirit to help you feel God's love. If you have never had this experience of the Holy Spirit filling your innermost heart, I would encourage you simply to ask God to fill you now.

Paul has still more to say about God's love. He says that even when you were against him, he sent Jesus to die for you. "But *God demonstrates his own love for us* in this: While we were still sinners, Christ died for us." (v.8)

This is how you know God loves you. The Father allowed his only Son to be taken from his embrace and sent to the cross. Even though we did not deserve it – we were ungodly sinners – Jesus died for us. God did not spare his own son. He loves you that much.

If God loves you so much, you can be certain that your future is secure. "If, when we were at our worst, we were put on friendly terms with God by the sacrificial death of his Son, now that we're at our best, just think of how our lives will expand and deepen by means of his resurrection life!" (v.10, MSG)

Lord, thank you so much that you died for me. Thank you that you love me so much and therefore I can be confident about my future. I ask that you would again pour your love into my heart by the Holy Spirit, and help me to feel your deep love for me.

Old Testament
Amos 6:1–7:17
3. God's love and grief

Do you know that God's anger is nothing but love? Here we see an example of that. God's anger is directed towards "complacent" leaders (6:1):

"Woe to those who live in luxury
    and expect everyone else to serve them!

Woe to those who live only for today,
 indifferent to the fate of others!
Woe to the playboys, the playgirls,
 who think life is a party held just for them!
Woe to those addicted to feeling good – life
without pain!
 those obsessed with looking good – life
without wrinkles!
They could not care less
 about their country going to ruin."
(vv.4–6, MSG)

It is not so much that they enjoy the good
things of life—none of which are sinful in
themselves. Rather, it is because they don't
care about the state of the people of God. God
hates pride and arrogance (vv.6,8) that fails to
acknowledge our need of him and keeps us from
experiencing his love for us and loving others as
he loves them.

If the leaders had loved God's people, as God
loved them, they would have grieved over their
country going to ruin.
Amos was an example of someone who did care
and did do something. He interceded for the
people. (7:1–6)

Amos was an ordinary person: "I never set
up to be a preacher, never had plans to be a
preacher. I raised cattle and I pruned trees. Then
God took me off the farm and said, 'Go preach
to my people Israel.'" (vv.14–15, MSG) God was

not content to simply watch injustice flourish. He loved his people too much for that. He raised up Amos to warn them of the consequences of what they were doing and to call them to turn back to his ways.

Like Amos, we want to pray and intercede for our nation:

"Sovereign Lord, forgive!" (v.2) In your great love, have mercy upon us. Thank you that you love your church and that you have power to bring life to the dead (Romans 4:24). Lord, we pray that you would raise up more people who hear your words and speak them with courage, power and love.

Pippa Adds
Amos 6:4a

"You lie on beds inlaid with ivory and lounge on your couches."

The chance would be a fine thing!

Notes:

Raniero Cantalamessa, *Life in Christ*, (Liturgical Press, 2002) p.7.

Robbie Williams and Guy Chambers, 'Feel', from *Escapology*, (Chrysalis, 2002)

If you would like more information about Alpha, please contact the following.

Alpha USA
1635 Emerson Lane
Naperville, IL 60540

800.362.5742
212.406.5269

info@alphausa.org
alphausa.org
alpharesources.org

@alphausa

Alpha in the Caribbean
Holy Trinity Brompton
Brompton Road
London SW7 1JA UK

+44 (0) 845.644.7544

americas@alpha.org
caribbean.Alpha.org

@AlphaCaribbean

Alpha Canada
Suite #230
11331 Coppersmith Way
Richmond, BC V7A 5J9

800.743.0899

office@alphacanada.org
alphacanada.org

Purchase resources in Canada:

Parasource
Canada
P.O. Box 98, 55 Woodslee Avenue
Paris, ON N3L 3E5

800.263.2664

custserv@parasource.com
parasource.com

Other Helpful Resources by Nicky Gumbel

Questions of Life goes into greater detail concerning the relevance of Jesus to our lives today.

Searching Issues provides biblical answers to seven key questions.

The Jesus Lifestyle is a study of the Sermon on the Mount.

30 Days is a practical introduction to reading the Bible.

Bible In One Year

"My favorite way to start the day."
Bear Grylls, Adventurer

"My heart leaps every morning when I see Bible in One Year by @nickygumbel sitting in my inbox."
Darlene Zschech, Worship Leader

No smartphone?

Subscribe at bibleinoneyear.org

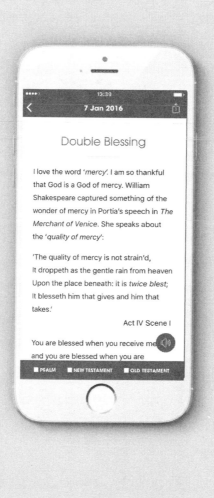